The Sustainable Living Book: Simple Steps to Build an Eco-Friendly Home and Lifestyle

Sustainable Living For beginners: tips and actionable steps to create a greener, more sustainable way of life

Jade M Emerson

Contents

Welcome to the Wild World of Sustainable Living ... v

1. UNDERSTANDING SUSTAINABILITY – SAVING THE PLANET WITHOUT LOSING YOUR COOL ... 1
   The Three Pillars of Sustainability: A Love Triangle That Actually Works ... 1
   Busting Sustainability Myths: Spoiler Alert, You *Can* Have Nice Things ... 2
   Critical Metrics for Measuring Your Eco-Awesomeness ... 3

2. ZERO-WASTE LIVING – BECAUSE TRASH DOESN'T NEED FRIENDS ... 5

3. SUSTAINABLE FASHION – LOOK GOOD, SAVE THE PLANET, REPEAT ... 10
   The Problem with Fast Fashion: It's Not Just About Ugly Christmas Sweaters ... 10
   Building a Conscious Wardrobe: Channel Your Inner Fashion Icon ... 11
   Clothing Care and Longevity: The Lazy Person's Guide to Saving the Planet ... 12

4. ECO-FRIENDLY ENERGY USE – POWER UP WITHOUT POWERING DOWN THE PLANET ... 14
   Understanding Energy Use and Your Carbon Footprint ... 14
   Exploring Renewable Energy: The Cool Stuff ... 16

5. URBAN GARDENING – HOW TO TURN A CONCRETE JUNGLE INTO AN EDIBLE PARADISE ... 18
   Even Your Balcony Can Be a Farm: The Basics of Growing Food in Small Spaces ... 18

6. INTRODUCTION TO PERMACULTURE –
GARDENING LIKE A GENIUS, NOT A GARDENER 21
What Is Permaculture? (Spoiler: It's More Than Just
Planting Stuff) 21

7. OFF-GRID LIVING – FREEDOM, SUSTAINABILITY,
AND A TINY BIT OF DIRT UNDER YOUR NAILS 25
Exploring the Possibilities of Off-Grid Living 25

8. SUSTAINABLE FOOD CHOICES – EATING YOUR
WAY TO A BETTER PLANET 29
Reducing Food Waste: Because Every Bite Counts 29
Understanding Labels and Certifications: Decoding
the Mystery 31

9. GETTING THERE WITHOUT COSTING THE
EARTH WITH GREEN TRANSPORTATION 33
The Impact of Transportation on the Environment:
Yes, Your Car Is Watching You 33
Exploring Electric Vehicles 35

10. BUILDING A SUSTAINABLE COMMUNITY –
BECAUSE SAVING THE PLANET TAKES A VILLAGE 37
Advocacy and Education: Be the Change, and Then
Inspire Others 37

11. MEASURING AND GROWING YOUR IMPACT –
CRUNCHING NUMBERS, CRUSHING GOALS 41
Tracking Your Sustainability Progress: Metrics
Without the Math Headache 41
Setting Long-Term Goals: Because Saving the Planet
Is a Marathon, Not a Sprint 42

Appendix I : 30-Day Action Plan 45
Appendix II : Step-by-Step Guides for DIY Eco-
Friendly Household Items and more! 49
Appendix III: Interactive Tools 55

Welcome to the Wild World of Sustainable Living

Congratulations! You've just picked up a book that promises to transform you from a waste-making, energy-guzzling, fast-fashion-loving mortal into an eco-warrior extraordinaire. Okay, maybe not overnight—but you'll undoubtedly make strides toward a kinder life for the planet, your wallet, and possibly even your sanity.

What *Exactly* Is Sustainable Living?

Sustainable living is about reducing lifestyle choices' negative effect on the environment. Think of it as being a thoughtful roommate to Planet Earth—turning off the lights, washing your own dishes (metaphorically speaking), and not throwing a raging trash party every week. It's about finding a balance between what you take and what you give back. And no, it doesn't mean living in a yurt and surviving solely on kale smoothies (unless you're into that, in which case, no judgment).

Why Should You Care? (Spoiler: It's a Big Deal)

Here's the thing: Earth's a bit stressed out. Climate change, over-

Welcome to the Wild World of Sustainable Living

flowing landfills, disappearing species—it's like the planet is hosting the worst house party ever, and we're the unruly guests. Sustainable living isn't just about hugging trees (though that's a bonus); it's about ensuring there's still a planet to host us 50 years from now. Plus, it can save money, simplify your life, and give you an impressive new hobby to brag about at dinner parties.

What's in It for You?

Here's the real kicker: sustainable living isn't just good for the Earth—it's excellent for you, too. Want to cut your utility bills in half? Sustainable living. Want a wardrobe so chic it could shame Paris Fashion Week? Sustainable living. Want to sleep better knowing you're doing your bit to save baby polar bears? You guessed it: sustainable living.

Oh, and did I mention it's fun? You'll be making your own cleaning products, upcycling old furniture, and growing tomatoes in places you didn't even know tomatoes could grow. By the time you finish this book, you'll be the MacGyver of sustainability.

How to Use This Guide Without Losing Your Mind

This book is your ultimate survival kit for the sustainability jungle. Each chapter focuses on a specific area of your life—like waste reduction, eco-friendly energy, and even sustainable fashion (yes, you can save the planet *and* look fabulous). You'll find actionable tips, beginner-friendly projects, and enough humour to keep things interesting. At the end, there's a 30-day plan that pulls everything together into bite-sized steps so you don't get overwhelmed and retreat into a Netflix binge.

A Sneak Peek at the 30-Day Sustainable Living Plan

This isn't a "read it and forget it" book. Oh no. When you hit the appendix, you'll be ready to dive into a month-long adventure that turns your newfound knowledge into real-life habits. You'll start

Welcome to the Wild World of Sustainable Living

small—maybe ditching plastic bags or mastering the art of composting—and by day 30, you'll be practically glowing with eco-friendly pride (and perhaps a little dirt under your nails).

Understanding Sustainability – Saving the Planet Without Losing Your Cool

Welcome to the foundation of sustainable living—the "Sustainability 101" class you never knew you needed. Don't worry; there are no pop quizzes, but there *will* be plenty of "Aha!" moments, possibly accompanied by guilty flashbacks to when you threw a soda can into the trash. Let's dive in.

The Three Pillars of Sustainability: A Love Triangle That Actually Works

First, we need to discuss the three pillars of sustainability—environmental, economic, and social. Think of them as the Avengers of eco-consciousness, working together to save the planet.

1 Environmental Sustainability

This one's the show's star—the group's Captain Planet. It's all about using resources without destroying them. That means fewer trees are getting turned into junk mail, and more renewable energy is used to keep your Netflix marathons guilt-free.

2 Economic Sustainability

Before you roll your eyes, this isn't about saving the world by buying more stuff. Quite the opposite, actually. Economic sustainability is about creating systems that make financial sense *and* don't trash the planet. Picture a world where supporting small businesses and saving money on your electric bill makes you an eco-hero. Win-win, right?

3 Social Sustainability

This is the people-focused pillar—like the friendly neighbour who lends you a cup of sugar (organic, of course). Social sustainability is about fairness, equality, and ensuring no one gets left behind. At the same time, we all try to save the world. It's basically the human side of being green.

Together, these three pillars form the basis of a sustainable lifestyle. They're like the ultimate squad goals, except they won't judge you for forgetting to bring your reusable straw.

Busting Sustainability Myths: Spoiler Alert, You *Can* Have Nice Things

Now that you're nodding along with the pillars let's address the elephant in the room: sustainability myths. They're like nasty rumours, except instead of high school drama, they stop people from helping the planet.

- **MYTH #1: Sustainability Is Just for Rich People**
  - False. Sustainable living isn't about dropping a fortune on organic bamboo pyjamas. It's about making intelligent, often cheaper choices—like mending your clothes instead of replacing them or eating leftovers instead of ordering takeout for the third night.

- **MYTH #2: You Have to Be Perfect**
  - Ha! No one's perfect. If you accidentally use a plastic fork at a

barbecue, the sustainability police won't come for you. (They're busy composting their veggie scraps.) The goal is progress, not perfection.

- **MYTH #3: It's Too Hard**
  - Sure, if your idea of sustainable living involves growing all your food and weaving your own clothes, then yes, that sounds exhausting. But for the rest of us, it's about simple, manageable steps—like switching to LED bulbs or carpooling with your coworkers. Easy peasy.

WHY YOU, Yes YOU, Are a Big Deal in This Fight

If you've ever thought, "What difference can one person make?" let me stop you. One person can do a *lot*. Remember, it wasn't a committee of squirrels that invented single-use plastics—it was humans. So, if we create a mess, we can clean it up.

Here's the thing: small actions add up. Imagine if everyone in your town stopped buying bottled water or used reusable shopping bags. That's a lot of plastic saved. Now imagine that multiplied by millions of people. See? You *do matter*.

Critical Metrics for Measuring Your Eco-Awesomeness

Alright, data nerds, this part's for you. How do you know if you're actually making a difference? Enter sustainability metrics.

- **Carbon Footprint**

Think of this as your environmental shadow. Everything you do—driving, eating, heating your home—leaves a carbon footprint. The goal? Shrink it. Like, baby-footprint small.

- **Waste Reduction**

How much trash are you sending to the landfill? If you're not sure, take a peek into your garbage can. (But maybe hold your breath.) Less trash = more eco points.

- **Water Usage**

Are you showering like you're in a shampoo commercial, or are you mindful of water conservation? Pro tip: shorter showers benefit the planet *and* your water bill.

- **Energy Consumption**

Check your energy usage. Those blinking lights on your electronics might as well be blinking "wasteful." Time to unplug and chill —literally.

Homework (But Fun, I Promise)

Before heading to the next chapter, here's a little challenge: Pick one sustainability myth to bust in your life this week. Maybe you'll start bringing your own mug to the coffee shop or finally commit to sorting your recycling.

And remember, you're not alone in this. Every great movement starts with individuals doing their part. So go forth and start flexing those eco-friendly muscles. You've got this!

Zero-Waste Living – Because Trash Doesn't Need Friends

Welcome to the world of zero-waste living, where the end goal is to send nothing to the landfill. By the end of this chapter, you'll be a waste-busting wizard armed with tips and tricks to minimize trash and maximize your eco-awesomeness.

What Is Zero-Waste Living? (And Why Should You Care?)

Imagine this: every piece of trash you've ever tossed is still somewhere, hanging around like that awkward party guest who won't leave. Zero-waste living is all about politely but firmly breaking up with that guest. It's about finding ways to reduce, reuse, and recycle so effectively that you hardly make any waste at all.

Reducing Household Waste: Baby Steps to Trash Freedom

Let's start with the basics. Cutting down on waste doesn't mean going full pioneer and making your own toothpaste out of tree bark. It's about making small swaps that, together, will make a big difference.

DIY AND RECIPES That Do Actually Work

Why spend money on chemical-laden cleaners when you can make your own with ingredients you already have? Behold, the dynamic duo: vinegar and baking soda.

ALL-PURPOSE CLEANER RECIPE:
- 1 cup of water and vinegar each
- A few drops of essential oil of your liking

Shake everything together, and voilà! You've got a cleaner that costs pennies and doesn't come in a single-use plastic bottle.

- **DITCH PAPER TOWELS for cloth rags.** Old T-shirts make excellent cleaning rags. Bonus points if the shirt has an embarrassing slogan.

- **INVEST IN REUSABLE CONTAINERS.** Glass jars are basically the MVPs of zero-waste living. They can hold leftovers, organize your pantry, or even serve as a trendy iced coffee cup if you're feeling fancy.

- **SAY NO TO SINGLE-USE PLASTICS.** Plastic bags? Out. Reusable shopping bags? In. They're less likely to rip open on your way home from the store.

. . .

STARTING and Maintaining Composting might sound like something farmers do. Still, even city folks can get in on the action. Think of it as a magical process where your veggie scraps turn into plant food instead of rotting in a landfill.

HOW TO START Your Compost Bin:

1 Get a bin. It can be a fancy tumbler or just an old bucket with holes.

2 Toss in your "greens" (food scraps) and "browns" (dry leaves, paper).

3 Stir a few times like it's a giant eco-friendly stew.

4 Wait for nature to do its thing.

PRO TIP: Avoid putting meat or dairy in your compost unless you want to invite some very enthusiastic raccoons to dinner.

CREATIVE REUSE AND UPCYCLING: Trash to Treasure

This is where zero-waste gets fun. Upcycling is like giving your old stuff a glow-up—it's the makeover montage of sustainable living.

BEESWAX WRAPS: The Hero Your Leftovers Deserve

Tired of wrestling with plastic wrap? Make your own beeswax wraps! All you need is some fabric, beeswax, and patience.

1 Cut your fabric into squares.
2 Brush melted beeswax onto the fabric.
3 Let it cool, and boom—you've got a reusable food cover that's both eco-friendly and Instagram-worthy.

UP YOUR DÉCOR

- **Turn mason jars into chic home décor.** Add fairy lights for an easy centrepiece, or use them to store random knick-knacks you can't bring yourself to part with.

SHOPPING MINDFULLY: The Jedi Mind Trick of Zero-Waste

When it comes to shopping, the key is to channel your inner minimalist. Before buying anything, ask yourself:

1 Do I really need this?
2 Can I get it secondhand?
3 Is it packaged in something that won't haunt future generations?

If the answer to all three is a resounding "yes," proceed. Otherwise, won't back and walk away like the zero-waste legend you're becoming.

The Sustainable Living Book: Simple Steps to Build an Eco-Friendly Ho...

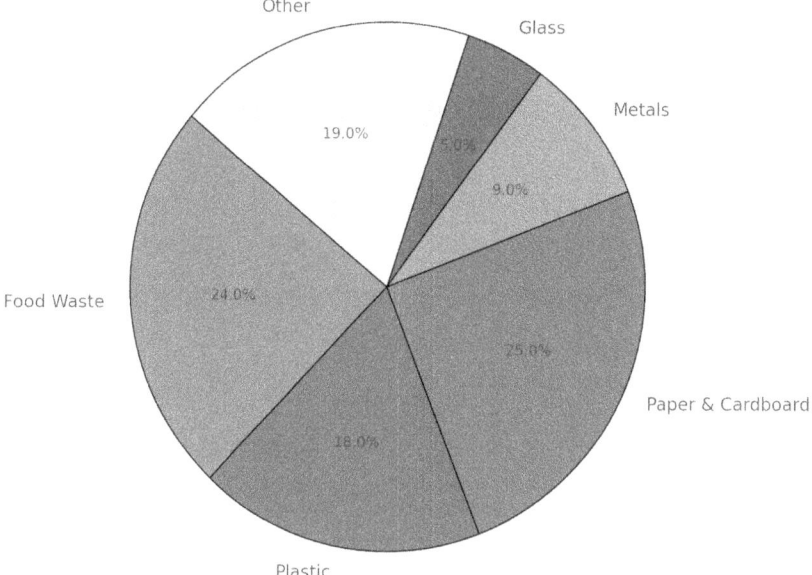

Here is an infographic-style pie chart illustrating the **Composition of Landfill Waste**, *showing the percentage contribution of various materials like food waste, plastic, and paper. This visual emphasizes the importance of reducing and reusing to minimize waste sent to landfills.*

Sustainable Fashion – Look Good, Save the Planet, Repeat

Welcome to the glamorous side of sustainability: fashion. That's right, your closet can be a force for good. Say goodbye to fast fashion that falls apart faster than a rom-com relationship, and hello to a wardrobe as kind to the Earth as it is to your sense of style. Get ready to turn your closet into an eco-fabulous shrine without sacrificing your flair for a killer outfit.

The Problem with Fast Fashion: It's Not Just About Ugly Christmas Sweaters

Fast fashion is the Kardashian of the sustainability world: it's everywhere, dramatic, and not great for the planet. Here's the tea:

1 It's Cheap, But Not Cheerful

Fast fashion thrives on producing trendy, low-cost clothes faster than you can say "next-day shipping." The catch? These clothes are made cheaply, often by underpaid workers, and fall apart after a few washes. No bueno.

2 The Environmental Price Tag

Every $5 T-shirt costs the planet big time. Think of massive water usage, toxic dyes, and piles of discarded clothing clogging up landfills. It's basically a disaster dressed up as a deal.

3 The Never-Ending Cycle

Fast fashion is new trends that arrives before we had change to wear last week's "must-have." It's like an endless buffet of bad decisions—except instead of overeating, we're over-consuming.

Building a Conscious Wardrobe: Channel Your Inner Fashion Icon

The good news? You don't have to swear off fashion altogether. Building a conscious wardrobe is like assembling the ultimate capsule collection—chic, timeless, and sustainable.

How to Create a Capsule Wardrobe Without Crying

The capsule wardrobe is a collection of high quality versatile pieces that mix and match effortlessly. The result? Fewer clothes, more outfits, and way less stress in the morning.

1 Audit Your Closet

Go through your wardrobe like you're auditioning each piece for a reality show. If it doesn't fit, flatter, or spark joy, it's out. But don't toss it—donate or upcycle it.

2 Invest in Staples

Think timeless, not trendy. A little black dress with a classic blazer will outlast every TikTok trend.

3 Add Some Personality

Accessories are your best friend. A statement scarf or bold earrings can elevate even the most basic outfit.

Thrifting and Shopping Secondhand Like a Pro

Thrifting is like a treasure hunt, except instead of gold doubloons, you find vintage jackets and gently-used designer boots. Here's how to score big:

- **Go in with a Plan.** Know what you're looking for a denim jacket or a funky pair of boots.
- **Check for Quality.** Avoid items with stains, tears, or that mysterious thrift store smell that just won't quit.
- **Get Creative.** Don't limit yourself to your usual size or section—oversized shirts and men's jackets can be goldmines.

Clothing Care and Longevity: The Lazy Person's Guide to Saving the Planet

Want to make your clothes last longer? Treat them like the VIPs they are. Here's how:

BASICS OF SEWING AND MENDING: Yes, You Can Fix That

You don't need to be a contestant on *The Great British Sewing Bee* to mend your clothes. Even the most hopeless seamstress can handle a basic repair:

- **Holes in Socks?** Learn the art of darning. Bonus: you'll sound fancy saying "darning."
- **Missing Buttons?** Sew them back on with a needle, thread, and the confidence of someone who just saved $20.

REFRESHING ACCESSORIES: From Drab to Fab

Tired of your old bag or shoes? Give them a new lease on life with some DIY love:

- **Polish leather accessories** with a homemade mixture of olive oil and vinegar.
- **Revamp old totes** with fabric paint or embroidery.

. . .

SUSTAINABLE CRAFTING TECHNIQUES: Fashion Meets Fun

Unleash your inner craft queen with these eco-friendly projects:

Natural Dyeing Using Plants and Food Waste

That beet juice you spilt on your shirt? Turns out, it's a fashion opportunity. Natural dyes from plants and food scraps are sustainable, safe, and relaxed.

1 Boil your chosen plant (beets, onion skins, avocado pits—yes, really) in water.

2 Submerge your fabric and let it soak.

3 Rinse, dry, and marvel at your one-of-a-kind creation.

UPCYCLING OLD CLOTHES Into New Designs

Got a shirt that's seen better days? Transform it:

- **Crop it.** Everything looks cooler cropped.
- **Turn it into a tote bag.** Google "T-shirt tote tutorial," and prepare to feel like a sewing genius.
- **Add patches or embroidery.** It's easier than you think and hides those unfortunate coffee stains.

TYING It All Back to the 30-Day Plan

Sustainable fashion doesn't happen overnight but doesn't need to be overwhelming. Start small: pick one habit to adopt, like thrifting or learning to sew. In the 30-day guide, Days 11, 12, and 22 will walk you through beginner-friendly steps, like building a capsule wardrobe or trying your hand at upcycling.

Eco-Friendly Energy Use – Power Up Without Powering Down the Planet

Let's talk about energy—no, not your caffeine addiction or the fact that your dog seems to have an endless supply of it. We're talking about the kind of energy that powers your home, charges your gadgets, and (unfortunately) contributes to the climate crisis. But don't worry—you don't have to go full caveman and start lighting your house with candles. By the end of this chapter, you'll know how to keep the lights on *and* the planet happy.

Understanding Energy Use and Your Carbon Footprint

First things first: what's a carbon footprint, and why does it matter? Picture every watt of electricity you use as leaving a tiny, smudgy footprint on the Earth. Multiply that by billions of people, and suddenly, Earth's looking like a muddy soccer field after a rainstorm. The goal? Shrink those footprints down to ballerina-on-her-tiptoes small.

How? Understanding where your energy comes from and how to

use less of it. Hint: it's easier than convincing your dog to stop barking at the mailman.

Making Your Home Energy Efficient: Lazy Hacks for Big Results

Let's face it: no one wants to spend hours figuring out how to save energy. Luckily, you don't have to. Here are some quick wins to make your home eco-friendly without cramping your style.

DIY Insulation and Weatherproofing Tips

Your home might be losing energy faster than a teenager loses interest in chores. Here's how to plug the leaks:

- **Draft-Proof Your Doors and Windows**
- Feel a chilly breeze coming from that window? Grab a weather-stripping kit and seal it up. No fancy tools are required.
- **Insulate Like a Pro**
- Adding insulation to your attic is like giving your house a cosy sweater. Bonus: it'll keep you warm in winter and cool in summer.

Reducing Phantom Power Consumption

Your electronics are sneaky little energy vampires, sucking power even when they're off. Fight back with these moves:

- **Unplug Appliances You're Not Using**
- If it's not in use, unplug it. Yes, even the toaster. Trust me, it doesn't need to stay plugged in overnight.
- **Use Power Strips**
- Get a power strip with an on/off switch to cut off power to multiple devices in one go.

Exploring Renewable Energy: The Cool Stuff

If you've ever dreamed of sticking it to your utility company, renewable energy is your chance. Here's how to make it work for you.

BASICS OF INSTALLING Solar Panels

Solar panels are like the ultimate DIY project for the planet. They sit on your roof, soak up the sunshine, and turn it into free (yes, *free*) energy. Here's the gist:

1 Call a professional. Seriously, climbing onto your roof with a screwdriver isn't the move.

2 Install panels in a sunny spot. (Sorry, Seattle friends.)

3 Bask in the glow of lower energy bills—and your eco-hero status.

SOLAR-POWERED GADGETS for Everyday Life

If rooftop panels aren't in your budget, try solar-powered gadgets. From phone chargers to outdoor lights, there's a solar-powered version of everything these days. Plus, they make great conversation starters. ("Oh, this flashlight? It's solar. No big deal.")

LOW-TECH ENERGY SOLUTIONS: When Simple Is Brilliant

Not every energy solution needs to be high-tech. Sometimes, the old-school stuff works just fine.

PASSIVE HEATING and Cooling Techniques

Here are a few clever tricks to keep your home comfortable:

- **Use Curtains Wisely**

Open them during the day to let in the sun's warmth and close them at night to trap them inside. Instant heating system.

• **Plant Shade Trees**

A strategically placed tree can block the sun in summer, keeping your house cooler. Plus, trees are fantastic, so why not?

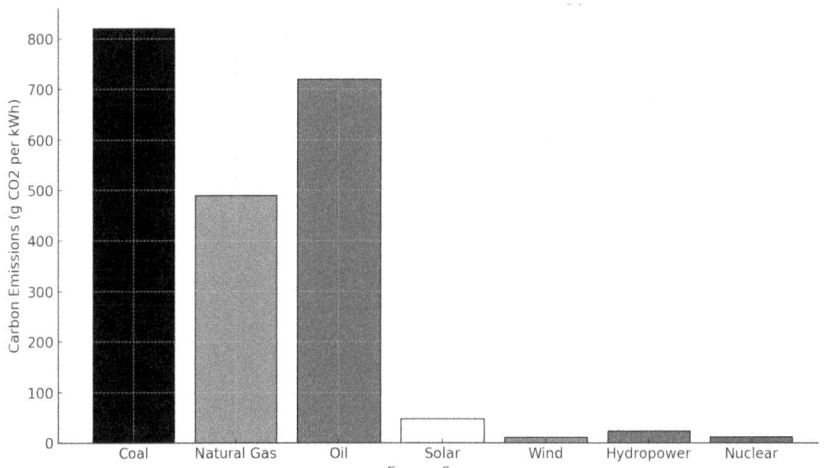

The **Carbon Emissions of Various Energy Sources** in grams of CO_2 per kilowatt-hour. This graphic compares traditional fossil fuels to renewable energy sources like solar, wind, and hydropower, emphasising the environmental benefits of clean energy.

Tying It All Back to the 30-Day Plan

Feeling inspired? Good, because you're about to become the CEO of your home's energy department. In the 30-day guide, Days 15–17 and 25 focus on practical energy-saving steps, like switching to LED bulbs, unplugging energy vampires, and exploring renewable energy options. Take it one day at a time, and soon you'll be running a lean, green, energy-saving machine.

Urban Gardening – How to Turn a Concrete Jungle into an Edible Paradise

Gardening in the city might sound like trying to grow tomatoes in a parking lot, but trust me, it's not only possible—it's a total game changer. Urban gardening is all about proving that you don't need acres of farmland to grow your own food.

Even Your Balcony Can Be a Farm: The Basics of Growing Food in Small Spaces

Don't have a yard? No problem. Urban gardening is like a puzzle: you just need to figure out how to fit your plants into your space. Whether it's a windowsill, balcony, or rooftop, there's always room for a little greenery.

Container Gardening: Plants Love Buckets Too

If you've got a pot, you've got a garden. Container gardening is the MVP of urban planting, and here's why:

- **Portable Plants**

• Containers let you move your plants to chase the sunlight. Lazy plants? Maybe. Genius? Definitely.

- **No Weeds, No Worries**

• Growing in containers means you won't spend your weekends battling weeds. Your back will thank you.

- **Perfect for Beginners**

• Start with easy-to-grow plants like cherry tomatoes, basil, or lettuce. They're practically foolproof, even if you've got a black thumb.

VERTICAL GARDENING: Because Walls Need Love Too

Running out of horizontal space? Go vertical. Use hanging baskets, wall planters, or even a shoe organizer to grow herbs and flowers. Bonus: it looks super Pinterest-worthy.

PEST CONTROL AND SOIL HEALTH: Keeping Your Plants Happy Without Waging War

Once you've got your garden growing, you might run into some uninvited guests. Don't worry—there are eco-friendly ways to deal with them.

ECO-FRIENDLY PEST MANAGEMENT

Forget toxic sprays. Fight pests the natural way, like the urban gardening ninja you are:

- **Invite the Good Guys** Ladybugs and praying mantises are your BFFs—they eat the bad bugs for you.
- **DIY Pest Sprays** Mix garlic and dish soap with water, spray it on your plants, and watch pests rethink their life choices.
- **Use Companion Planting** Plant marigolds near your veggies to deter pests. They're like the bodyguards of the plant world.

· · ·

COMPOST INTEGRATION: YOUR PLANTS' Favorite Snack

Remember that compost bin you started in Chapter 2? Now it's time to use it. Mix compost into your soil for a nutrient boost that'll make your plants do a happy dance. (Okay, not literally, but you'll see the results.)

COMMUNITY GARDENING: Because Growing Together Is Better

Urban gardening doesn't have to be a solo act. Joining—or starting—a community garden can turn your green thumb into a full-blown movement.

Joining a Community Garden

Community gardens are like the co-working spaces of gardening. You get a plot, some tools, and a chance to swap tips (and maybe zucchinis) with your neighbors.

Starting Your Own Garden Project

No community garden nearby? Start one! Gather a group of like-minded people, find a neglected patch of land, and turn it into a green oasis. Pro tip: start small and get permission before you dig up that random lot.

URBAN GARDENING and the 30-Day Plan: Your Green Thumb on a Schedule

In the 30-day guide, Days 18, 24, and 28 are all about urban gardening. You'll get step-by-step instructions for starting small, whether it's planting herbs in a mason jar or trying your hand at vertical gardening. By the end of the month, you'll be well on your way to becoming your neighborhood's go-to garden guru.

Introduction to Permaculture – Gardening Like a Genius, Not a Gardener

Welcome to permaculture, the art and science of working *with* nature instead of waging a passive-aggressive war against it. It's not just about gardening—it's about creating self-sustaining ecosystems that practically take care of themselves. Think of it as the lazy gardener's dream: maximum impact with minimum effort. Ready to become one with nature? Let's dig in.

What Is Permaculture? (Spoiler: It's More Than Just Planting Stuff)

At its core, permaculture is about designing your life and landscape to mimic how nature works. You're essentially trying to outsmart Mother Nature by copying her homework. It's all about using natural principles to create productive, self-sufficient, and eco-friendly systems.

The Core Principles and Ethics of Permaculture

1 Earth Care - Translation: Don't trash the planet. Use resources responsibly and think about the long-term health of the environment.

2 People Care - Be nice to yourself and others. Create systems that support communities and well-being.

3 Fair Share - Share what you have, and don't hoard all the resources. Even the squirrels know this one.

Understanding Zoning and Basic Design

Permaculture isn't just about throwing seeds everywhere and hoping for the best. It's a carefully planned operation with zones designed to save you time and effort:

- **Zone 1:** Stuff you use daily, like herbs or veggies, goes near your house.
- **Zone 2:** Less frequent maintenance, like fruit trees, a chicken coop, or a compost pile.
- **Zone 3:** Things that need even less attention, like a wildflower meadow or crops that grow like weeds.
- **Zone 4:** Semi-wilderness, like a forest or foraging area (if you're fancy).
- **Zone 5:** Pure wilderness. Think of it as nature's VIP lounge—no humans allowed.

Permaculture Projects for Beginners: Start Small, Think Big

Permaculture might sound overwhelming, but it's all about starting small and letting nature do most of the work.

Creating Food Forests and Perennial Gardens

A food forest is like a buffet but for you and the wildlife. It's a layered system of trees, shrubs, and ground plants that all work together:

1 **Canopy Layer:** Fruit and nut trees.
2 **Understory:** Smaller trees, like dwarf varieties.
3 **Shrub Layer:** Berries and currants.
4 **Herbaceous Layer:** Herbs, veggies, and flowers.
5 **Ground Cover:** Clover, strawberries, or other low-growers.
6 **Root Layer:** Potatoes, carrots, and other underground treasures.
7 **Vertical Layer:** Vines like grapes or beans.

Once it's established, it practically takes care of itself. You'll be sipping lemonade in the shade of your apple tree while your food forest does all the work.

Water Harvesting Techniques: Because Every Drop Counts

Permaculture loves water more than a toddler with a garden hose. Here are some beginner-friendly ways to save and use it wisely:

- **Swales:** Fancy word for a ditch that slows and spreads water, helping it soak into the ground instead of running off.
- **Rain Gardens:** Plant a garden in a low spot where water naturally collects. The plants will love it, and you'll reduce runoff.
- **Rain Barrels:** Stick one under your downspout, and voilà! Free water for your plants.

Permaculture Beyond Gardening: Eco-Wisdom for Everyday Life

Permaculture isn't just for your yard—it's a mindset you can apply. Here's how:

. . .

- **Waste Less, Share More**
  - Swap leftovers with neighbours, start a tool-sharing group, or join a local "buy nothing" community.
- **Design Your Life Like a Permaculture Garden**
  - Prioritize what's important, put your resources where needed, and let go of what doesn't serve you.

Tying It All Back to the 30-Day Plan

On days 23 and 27 of the 30-day plan, you'll get hands-on with simple permaculture projects. Start by creating a mini food forest in your yard or balcony, or try a small-scale water harvesting project. It's easier than you think, and the results are gratifying (not to mention brag-worthy).

Off-Grid Living – Freedom, Sustainability, and a Tiny Bit of Dirt Under Your Nails

Welcome to off-grid living, where you become the boss of your energy, water, and waste systems.

Exploring the Possibilities of Off-Grid Living

Off-grid living isn't all Instagram-worthy sunsets - It's equally rewarding and challenging, but if you're up for the adventure, it's 100% worth it.

CHALLENGES AND REWARDS
The Challenges:

- You're responsible for energy, water, waste, and maintenance.
- It can be pricey upfront. Solar panels and water systems don't come cheap.
- Convenience takes a backseat. No Uber Eats in the middle of nowhere.

The Rewards:

- Freedom from utility bills.
- A deeper connection to nature.
- The ultimate bragging rights: It's all solar. No big deal."

ENERGY INDEPENDENCE: Powering Up Like a Pro

Be in charge of your own power. That might sound daunting, but with the proper setup, you'll binge-watch Netflix on solar energy in no time.

ADVANCED SOLAR and Wind Systems

1 Solar Panels: Install a system big enough to handle your energy needs and pair it with a battery bank to store power for cloudy days.

2 Wind Turbines: A wind turbine can complement your solar setup, giving you power even when the sun takes a break.

3 Backup Generators: Even the best systems can't predict a week of storms. A backup generator (ideally biofuel or propane) is your safety net.

SETTING Up a Sustainable Battery Bank

Your battery bank is like the pantry for your power—it stores energy so you can use it when the sun's not shining or the wind's not blowing. Opt for lithium-ion batteries if you can afford them—they're more efficient and last longer than lead-acid ones.

WATER AND WASTE SYSTEMS: Because Plumbing Matters

Living off-grid means controlling two essentials: water and waste. Don't worry; it's not as scary as it sounds.

RAINWATER HARVESTING and Filtration

Why rely on municipal water when the sky gives it away for free? Set up a rainwater collection system to capture and filter water for drinking, cooking, and washing.

1 Install gutters and a downspout that feed into a storage tank.
2 Use a first-flush diverter to keep debris out of your tank.
3 Purify the water to make it safe to drink.

GREYWATER Recycling

Don't let your used water go to waste. Grey water systems let you reuse water from sinks, showers, and washing machines for irrigation. Pro tip: stick to biodegradable soaps and detergents to keep your garden happy.

BUILDING ECO-FRIENDLY SHELTERS: Cozy, Green, and Gorgeous

If you're going off-grid, your home should reflect your sustainable values. Fortunately, plenty of options are as eco-friendly as they are stylish.

COB, Straw Bale, and Earth-ship Designs

- **Cob Houses:** Think of cob as fancy mud—clay, sand, and straw mixed together to create walls that are strong, breathable, and charmingly rustic.
- **Straw Bale Homes:** Insulate your home with straw bales

for a cosy, energy-efficient space. No, the Big Bad Wolf can't blow it down.

• **Earth-ships:** These futuristic homes are made from recycled materials like tyres and bottles and designed to be self-sufficient. Think of it as living in an eco-bunker.

Passive Solar Design Principles

Design your home to work with the sun and not against it. South-facing windows (Northern Hemisphere) let in warmth during winter, while overhangs keep things cool in summer. It's like free climate control.

Tying It All Back to the 30-Day Plan

Days 19 and 27 of the 30-day guide are your off-grid training wheels. Start by experimenting with rainwater collection or researching solar options.

Sustainable Food Choices – Eating Your Way to a Better Planet

Let's face it: food is life. Whether you're a salad lover, a pizza enthusiast, or someone who secretly eats cereal for dinner (we've all been there), the way you eat has a significant impact on the planet. But don't worry—you don't have to go full forager or live on kale smoothies to make sustainable food choices. This chapter will show you how to eat well, save the planet, and impress your friends with your newfound eco-foodie cred.

Reducing Food Waste: Because Every Bite Counts

Did you know one-third of all food produced worldwide is in the trash? That's like ordering three pizzas and tossing one straight into the garbage. Yikes. But fear not—reducing food waste is easier (and tastier) than you think.

Thoughtful Meal Planning and Storage Tips
1 Plan Like a Pro
Make a meal plan and stick to it before going to the grocery store.

No more buying random eggplants that rot in the fridge because you "thought you'd try something new."

2 Store Food Like a Scientist

Herbs stay fresher if stored in a glass of water, like a bouquet of leafy greatness. Use airtight containers to prevent leftovers from becoming science experiments.

3 The Freezer Is Your BFF

Got extra veggies, bread, or leftovers? Freeze them. Future you will be so grateful.

CREATIVE USES for Leftovers and Scraps

Turn food scraps into gold:

- **Vegetable Broth:** Save veggie scraps and make a delicious broth by boiling them.
- **Banana Bread:** Overripe bananas are a blessing in disguise—hello, banana bread.
- **Pickle Everything:** Leftover cucumbers, radishes, or even watermelon rinds? Pickle them. Trust me, it's a game-changer.

EAT LOCAL AND SEASONAL: Fresh, Tasty, and Planet-Friendly

Eating seasonally and locally is like dating the planet—it's all about paying attention to and appreciating what's available.

Navigating Farmer's Markets and CSAs

Farmers markets are a goldmine for seasonal, local produce. Here's how to make the most of them:

1 Go Early: The best stuff sells out fast.

2 Ask Questions: Farmers love to share tips about how to cook, store, or even grow what they're selling.

THE BENEFITS of Seasonal Eating

When you eat what's in season, you get fresher, tastier, and less resource-intensive food. Bonus: it's often cheaper because it didn't travel halfway around the world to get to your plate.

Understanding Labels and Certifications: Decoding the Mystery

Grocery shopping shouldn't require a degree in cryptography, but sometimes it feels like it does. Here's how to decode standard food labels:

- **Organic:** Grown without synthetic pesticides or fertilizers. A great choice, but not the only one.
- **Fair Trade:** Your morning coffee would be even better if you knew the farmers and workers who produced it were paid fairly.
- **Non-GMO:** No genetically modified ingredients. Great if you're worried about Franken-food.

Only some labels are a dealbreaker, but understanding them helps you make informed choices.

SUSTAINABLE PROTEIN CHOICES: Where's the Beef? (Or Not.)

Protein is essential, but it doesn't have to come at the planet's expense.

Plant-Based Options

Going plant-based even a few days a week can make a huge difference. Try lentils, chickpeas, or tofu—they're versatile, delicious, and won't judge you if you mess up the seasoning.

Sustainable Meat and Seafood

If you're not ready to give up meat, look for sustainably raised or caught options:

- **Grass-Fed Beef:** Better for the environment and the cows.

- **Wild-Caught Fish:** Choose species that aren't overfished (hint: avoid bluefin tuna).
- **Local and Pasture-Raised:** Support farmers in your area who treat animals ethically.

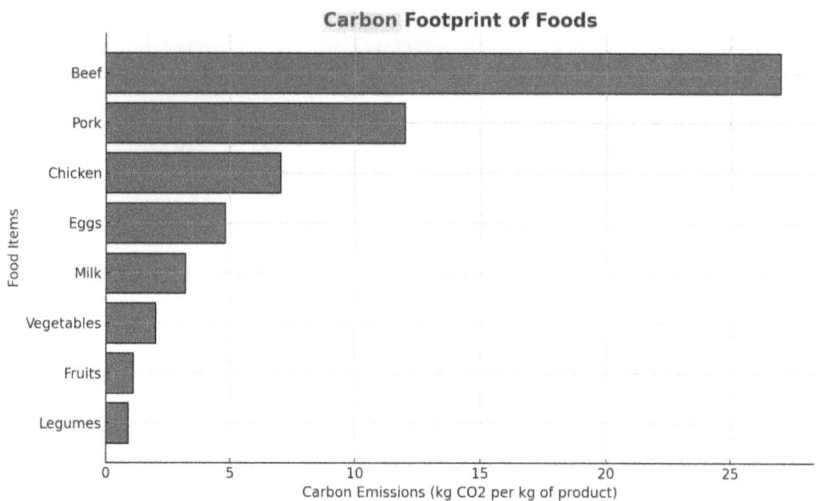

The **Carbon Footprint of Foods**, *with data representing the kilograms of CO_2 emitted per kilogram of various food products.*

Tying It All Back to the 30-Day Plan

You'll tackle sustainable eating head-on in Days 13 and 26 of the 30-day plan. From planning zero-waste meals to trying seasonal recipes, you'll get hands-on experience that's as delicious as it is impactful. Don't be surprised if you end up with a favorite farmer at the market or a new appreciation for lentils.

Getting There Without Costing the Earth With Green Transportation

Let's talk about transportation, modern life's unsung hero (or villain). Whether you're commuting, running errands, or embarking on a road trip, getting from Point A to Point B significantly impacts the planet. But don't worry—going green doesn't mean trading your car for a horse-drawn carriage. This chapter will explore practical ways to make your travels kinder to the environment without sacrificing convenience or style.

The Impact of Transportation on the Environment: Yes, Your Car Is Watching You

Transportation emissions are one of the most significant contributors to greenhouse gases. Planes, trains, and automobiles burn fossil fuels extensively.

The good news? Every little shift toward greener transportation helps. And no, you don't have to bike to work in a blizzard to make a difference.

. . .

Eco-Friendly Alternatives: Saving the Planet, One Ride at a Time

Let's explore some greener ways to get around—your wallet, your health, and the Earth will thank you.

Walking: The Original Green Transport

Walking isn't just good for the planet and your legs, lungs, and mood. Here's why it's worth considering:

- **Zero Emissions:** Unless you eat beans before your walk, you're as eco-friendly as possible.
- **Health Boost:** Burn calories, not fuel. It's the ultimate win-win.
- **Mindful Moments:** Walking gives you time to notice the world around you. Bonus: you'll finally know your neighbors' dog's name.

Cycling: Two Wheels, Infinite Benefits

Biking is like walking's cooler cousin. It's fast, fun, and great for the environment.

- **Commute Smarter:** Skip the traffic jams and zoom past cars like the eco-warrior you are.
- **Affordable:** Maintenance is way cheaper than gas or bus fares once you've got a bike.
- **Adventure-Ready:** Add a basket for groceries or panniers for a weekend getaway—no car required.

Public Transit: Sharing Is Caring

Do you need more time to give up motorized travel? Public transit is the next best thing.

- **Fewer Cars, Less Pollution:** Every person on a bus or train means one less car on the road.

• **Relax While You Ride:** Read, nap, or people-watch instead of yelling at traffic.

CARPOOLING: Ride Together, Save Together

Carpooling isn't just for kids on field trips. Find coworkers, friends, or neighbours heading your way and split the ride—and the cost. Bonus: fewer cars means less road rage.

Exploring Electric Vehicles

If you need a car, consider going electric. EVs (electric vehicles) are cleaner, quieter, and cooler than their gas-guzzling cousins.

BENEFITS OF EVs

1 **No Tailpipe Emissions:** EVs don't burn gas, which means cleaner air and fewer greenhouse gases.

2 **Lower Operating Costs:** EVs require less maintenance, and Electricity is cheaper than gas.

3 **Silent Rides:** Enjoy your favorite podcasts without engine noise ruining the vibe.

GETTING STARTED with EVs

• Research tax credits or rebates in your area—they can make EVs more affordable.

• If you can't commit to an EV, consider a hybrid. Baby steps count, too.

SUSTAINABLE TRAVEL: Greener Vacations and Trips

Travelling doesn't have to mean leaving a giant carbon footprint behind. Here's how to see the world without hurting it.

Tips for Eco-Friendly Vacations
• **Take the Train:** Trains are one of the greenest ways to travel long distances. Plus, they're weirdly romantic.

• **Pack Light:** Every pound on a plane increases fuel consumption. Leave the "just-in-case" outfits at home.

• **Stay Local:** Support eco-friendly accommodations and local businesses wherever you go.

Tying It All Back to the 30-Day Plan
In the 30-day guide, transportation tips appear from Day 1 onward. You'll start by rethinking your daily commute—walking or biking when you can—and work up to more significant changes.

So, lace up your sneakers, dust off your bike, or hop on the bus. The journey to a greener future starts with one ride.

Building a Sustainable Community – Because Saving the Planet Takes a Village

You've got your compost bin humming, your wardrobe looking fabulous in thrifted treasures, and your solar panels doing their sun-powered magic. Now it's time to level up your sustainability game by building a community as eco-awesome as you are. Think of it as taking your solo act and turning it into a band—because sustainability is way more fun (and practical) when you do it together.

Advocacy and Education: Be the Change, and Then Inspire Others

You don't have to be a professor or an Instagram influencer to inspire change. Sometimes, it's as simple as starting a conversation or sharing what you've learned.

Sharing Your Journey and Inspiring Others
- **Lead by Example:** Nothing says, "You can do this too," like showing people how easy (and cool) sustainable living can be. Invite

friends over for a zero-waste dinner or gift them homemade beeswax wraps.
- **Start Small Conversations:** Whether it's swapping recipes for DIY cleaners at a party or talking about your composting adventures at work, you'd be surprised how many people are curious about living green.
- **Get Social (Media):** Share your sustainability wins online, from upcycled projects to urban gardening hacks. Just be honest—no one's expecting perfection.

COLLABORATIVE LIVING: Sharing Is Caring (and Resource-Saving)

Humans have survived for thousands of years by working together—so why stop now?

SHARING Resources and Skills
- **Tool Libraries:** Why buy a drill you'll use once when you can borrow one?
- **Skill Swapping:** Trade your bread-baking skills for your neighbor's bike-repair expertise. It's like bartering but way cooler.

STARTING Eco-Initiatives

Whether it's a local clean-up group, or starting a a community garden, or an energy co-op, joining forces with others amplifies your impact. And hey, you might make some new friends along the way.

INVOLVING FUTURE GENERATIONS: The Kids Are Alright (and Adorable)

Want to future-proof your sustainability efforts? Get the kids involved. They'll be running the planet one day, so teaching them eco-friendly habits now is like planting seeds for a greener future.

Teaching Kids About Sustainability

- **Make It Fun:** Turn recycling into a game, or take them on a nature scavenger hunt.
- **Lead by Example:** Kids are like sponges—they'll notice if you practice what you preach.
- **Encourage Curiosity:** Answer their endless "why" questions about the environment. It's worth it, even if it tests your patience.

Building a Few Family-Friendly Eco Projects

- Create DIY bird feeders using old milk cartons or toilet paper rolls and watch the birds flock.
- Make a garden together: Even toddlers can help plant seeds or water flowers.
- Grab some gloves and a bag, and turn a walk into a clean-up mission.

Celebrating Community Success: Because You Deserve It

Building a sustainable community is hard work, but it's also gratifying. Don't forget to take a step back and celebrate your wins.

- **Host an Eco-Party:** Think potluck, but with sustainable flair—local ingredients, reusable dishes, and maybe even a compost station.
- **Share Stories:** Whether through a blog, a newsletter, or a chalkboard in the community garden.
- **Reflect and Set Goals:** What worked? What didn't?

Tie it Back to the 30-Day Plan

On days 28 and 30 of the above guide, you will dive into the community- reflection and community building. By then, you'll have a solid foundation of sustainable habits and the confidence to share them with others.

So get out there and start talking, sharing, and celebrating. We can turn the world into a giant, thriving, eco-friendly neighborhood. And really, isn't that what it's all about?

Measuring and Growing Your Impact – Crunching Numbers, Crushing Goals

Congratulations, you've made it to the final chapter! By now, you've tackled compost bins, rocked thrifted fashion, and maybe even considered going off-grid. But how do you know if all this effort makes a difference? Enter: measuring and growing your impact. It's like tracking your progress at the gym, but you're building a better planet instead of biceps.

Tracking Your Sustainability Progress: Metrics Without the Math Headache

You'll need some tools to track your eco-journey to see how far you've come. Don't worry—there won't be any pop quizzes, just a few simple ways to measure your awesomeness.

Tools for Measuring Your Carbon Footprint

Your carbon footprint is like a giant sneaker print stomping on the planet. The goal? Make it smaller. Here's how to track it:
- **Carbon Calculators:** Websites like Carbon Footprint and

CoolClimate let you input details about your lifestyle to estimate your emissions. It's like a diagnostic for your eco-life.
- **Utility Bills:** Check your energy usage over time. If it's trending down, you're winning.
- **Waste Tracking:** Take a peek in your trash can—if it's emptier than it was six months ago, you're on the right track.

Reflecting on Your Lifestyle Changes

Take a moment - consider where you started and how far you have come. Are you composting? Shopping locally? Walking instead of driving? These small shifts add up to big wins.

Setting Long-Term Goals: Because Saving the Planet Is a Marathon, Not a Sprint

Now that you've got the basics down, it's time to think bigger. What's next on your sustainability bucket list?

Sustainable Living Challenges

Challenge yourself (and maybe your friends) to up your eco-game. Here are some ideas to get you started:
- **Zero-Waste Month:** See how little trash you can create in 30 days. Spoiler: it's easier than it sounds.
- **Buy Nothing Challenge:** Spend a month buying only essentials like food. Get creative with what you already have.
- **Meatless Mondays (or More):** Dedicate a day—or a few days—to plant-based eating.

Reaching Milestones

Break your bigger goals into smaller ones:
- Save up for a solar panel installation by the end of the year.

• Convince one friend to join you on the sustainability journey. (Peer pressure, but make it eco-friendly.)

Tying It All Back to the 30-Day Plan

On Day 29, you'll take stock of your progress and set new goals. Consider it a sustainability tune-up: reflecting on what worked, identifying improvement areas, and planning your next steps.

Keep challenging yourself, and keep celebrating wins. You've come so far, and the best part? This journey never really ends. There's always more to learn, do, and share. And that's what makes it so exciting.

Now, go out there and show the world what a sustainable superstar looks like. Spoiler alert: it looks a lot like you.

Appendix 1 : 30-Day Action Plan

Week 1: The Foundation

Day 1: Map Your Sustainable Journey
  • Write down three goals for the next 30 days. Example: Reduce waste, save energy, eat more sustainably.

Day 2: Ditch the Plastic Bags
  • Replace disposable bags with reusable ones. Bonus: Make your own tote from an old T-shirt.

Day 3: Switch to Reusable Water Bottles and Coffee Cups
  • Say goodbye to single-use bottles and cups. (Your favorite coffee shop probably loves reusable mugs!)

Day 4: Start Making Compost
  • A Small compost bin can be used in the kitchen for all the food scraps. (Hint: See Chapter 2 for tips.)

Day 5: Master Meal Planning
  • Plan your meals for the week to reduce food waste and save time. Pro tip: Use leftovers creatively.

Day 6: Audit Your Trash

- Take a peek at your garbage can. Identify what you throw away most and brainstorm alternatives.

Day 7: Unplug Energy Vampires
- Identify devices that suck energy when not in use (hello, TV!) and unplug them.

Week 2: Waste Less, Save More

Day 8: Try DIY Cleaners
- Make your first batch of all-purpose cleaners. Bonus: Share your recipe with a friend.

Day 9: Cook a Zero-Waste Meal
- Use everything in your fridge. Scrappy soup, anyone?

Day 10: Make Beeswax Wraps
- Create your own reusable food wraps. (Chapter 2 has your back.)

Day 11: Explore Sustainable Fashion
- Visit a thrift store or try creating a capsule wardrobe.

Day 12: Learn Basic Mending Skills
- Sew a button, patch a hole, or hem some pants. (It's easier than you think!)

Day 13: Eat Seasonally and Locally
- Visit a farmer's market or cook a meal using local, seasonal ingredients.

Day 14: Conduct an Energy Audit
- Check your home for drafty windows, outdated bulbs, or inefficient appliances.

Week 3: Eco-Friendly Energy and Beyond

Day 15: Switch to LED Bulbs
- Replace old bulbs with energy-efficient LEDs. Bonus: They last forever (almost).

Day 16: Adjust Your Thermostat

Appendix 1 : 30-Day Action Plan

• Turn it down in winter and up in summer. Small changes = significant savings.

Day 17: Research Renewable Energy Options
• Look into solar panels or community solar programs in your area.

Day 18: Plant Something Green
• Start a small herb garden or plant flowers for pollinators. (See Chapter 5.)

Day 19: Experiment with Water-Saving Techniques
• Shorten showers, fix leaks, or install a low-flow showerhead.

Day 20: Use Public Transit or Carpool
• Reduce your transportation emissions by trying a greener commute.

Day 21: Go Paperless
• Opt for e-bills and digital statements. Less paper = fewer trees chopped down.

Week 4: Scaling Up and Sharing the Love

Day 22: Host a Clothing Swap
• Invite friends to swap clothes instead of buying new ones. Instant wardrobe refresh!

Day 23: Start a Mini Permaculture Project
• Create a small food forest or experiment with companion planting. (Chapter 6 has ideas.)

Day 24: Build a DIY Vertical Garden
• Maximize small spaces by growing up instead of out. Herbs, strawberries, or succulents work great.

Day 25: Reduce Phantom Energy Use
• Use power strips with on/off switches to easily control multiple devices.

Day 26: Try a Plant-Based Meal Day
• Dedicate a day to delicious vegetarian or vegan meals.

Day 27: Explore Off-Grid Living Tips

• Research rainwater harvesting or learn about solar-powered gadgets.

Day 28: Get Involved in Your Community
• Join a clean-up group, start a garden project, or advocate for local sustainability initiatives.

Week 5: Reflect, Refine, and Keep Growing

Day 29: Review and Set Long-Term Goals
• Reflect on your progress. What worked? What didn't? Set three new sustainability goals.

Day 30: Celebrate Your Eco-Journey
• Host a sustainable party, share your journey online, or take a moment to appreciate how far you've come.

Additional Resources: Your Sustainability Toolbox
• **Books and Guides:** Check out titles like *The Zero Waste Home* or *The Sustainable Living Handbook*.

• **Websites:** Explore sites like Earth911 and Energy.gov for tips and resources.

• **Apps:** Try apps like JouleBug or iRecycle to stay motivated and organized.

• **Checklists:** Create sustainability checklists to track progress and stay on track with your goals.

Progress, Not Perfection

This 30-day guide isn't about becoming the world's most eco-perfect person—it's about progress. No matter how small, every step you take is a step toward a healthier planet. And the best part? It doesn't stop here. Use this guide as a foundation to build your sustainable lifestyle, one awesome action at a time.

Now go forth, live greener, and inspire others to do the same. You've got this!

Appendix II : Step-by-Step Guides for DIY Eco-Friendly Household Items and more!

1. DIY Natural Cleaners
Project: All-Purpose Cleaner
Materials Needed:
- 1 cup white vinegar
- 1 cup water
- 1 lemon (optional, for scent)
- 10-15 drops of essential oil (e.g., tea tree or lavender)
- Spray bottle

Steps:
1 Mix water and vinegar in a bowl
2 Squeeze out the lemon juice forr extra cleaning power and fragrance.
3 Add 10-15 drops of essential oil for additional antibacterial properties and a pleasant smell.
4 Pour mixture into a spray bottle.
5 Use it on countertops, sinks, and other surfaces. Avoid using it on granite or marble, as vinegar may damage these surfaces.

2. DIY Compost Bin

Project: Indoor Compost Bin

Materials Needed:
- A bin with a lid (plastic or metal)
- Drill with a small drill bit
- Shredded paper, cardboard or other carbon materials
- Fruit peels, vegetable scraps or other nitrogen materials
- Soil

Steps:

1 Drill small holes in the bin's sides, lid, and bottom to allow for airflow.

2 Place a layer of carbon materials at the bottom of the bin.

3 Add a layer of nitrogen materials, such as fruit and vegetable scraps.

4 Cover the nitrogen layer with a thin layer of soil.

5 Alternate layers of carbon and nitrogen materials as you add more waste.

6 Stir the compost occasionally to aerate it and speed up decomposition.

7 Use the finished compost for gardening or potted plants.

3. Upcycled Decor

Project: Glass Jar Lanterns

Materials Needed:
- Empty glass jars (mason jars or old candle jars work well)
- Twine or wire
- LED tea lights or candles
- Decorative materials eg paint or glue

Steps:

1 Clean and dry the glass jars thoroughly.

2 Decorate the jars using paint, stickers, or other embellishments.

3 Wrap twine or wire around the mouth of the jar, leaving enough to create a loop for hanging.

4 Place an LED tea light or candle inside the jar.

Appendix II : Step-by-Step Guides for DIY Eco-Friendly Household Ite...

5 Hang the lanterns indoors or outdoors, or use them as table centerpieces.

Additional eco-friendly DIY project ideas:

Home & Kitchen DIY Projects

1 Reusable Beeswax Wraps
- Replace plastic wrap with reusable, moldable fabric wraps coated in beeswax.

2 Homemade Dish Soap
- A natural, chemical-free alternative to store-bought dish soaps.

3 Cloth Napkins from Old T-Shirts
- Upcycle old t-shirts into reusable napkins or cleaning cloths.

4 DIY Herb Garden
- Grow herbs on a balcony using mason jars, tin cans, or wooden boxes.

5 Eco-Friendly Sponges
- Craft sponges using natural loofah or crocheted jute fibers.

Cleaning & Organizing DIY Projects

1 Natural Laundry Detergent
- Create a powdered detergent using washing soda, borax, and grated soap.

2 Reusable Dryer Sheets
- Soak fabric scraps in a natural softener mixture to replace disposable dryer sheets.

3 Shoe Organizer from Cardboard
- Upcycle cardboard boxes into a modular, stackable shoe rack.

Gardening & Outdoor DIY Projects

1 Vertical Garden Planter
- Build a vertical garden for small spaces from pallets, gutters, or hanging pots.

2 Bird Feeder from Recycled Materials
- Use milk cartons, plastic bottles, or tin cans to create bird feeders.

3 DIY Rain Barrel
- Capture and store rainwater for outdoor use with a simple barrel and spout system.

4 Seed Starter Pots from Paper Rolls
- Recycle toilet paper rolls into biodegradable pots for seedlings.

Decor & Gift DIY Projects

1 Cork Board from Wine Corks
- Wine corks can be glued onto a board to create a functional, eco-friendly corkboard.

2 Candles from Leftover Wax
- Melt wax scraps to create new candles using recycled jars or tins.

3 Fabric Tote Bags
- Sew reusable shopping bags from old clothes or fabric remnants.

4 Decorative Storage Baskets
- Weave baskets using old newspapers or magazines.

Personal Care & Wellness DIY Projects

1 Homemade Lip Balm
- Mix beeswax, coconut, and essential oils for a moisturizing lip balm.

2 Reusable Makeup Remover Pads

Appendix II : Step-by-Step Guides for DIY Eco-Friendly Household Ite...

- Sew pads from soft fabric like flannel or bamboo cloth.

3 Bath Bombs
- Make bath bombs with baking soda, citric acid, and natural scents.

4 Herbal Sachets for Closets
- Fill small fabric bags with dried lavender or cedar shavings for natural moth repellents.

DIY Projects to Upcycle and Repurpose

1 Furniture Makeover with Paint
- Refinish old furniture to give it a modern, stylish look.

2 Mason Jar Soap Dispensers
- Convert mason jars into chic soap dispensers using pump tops.

3 DIY Rug from Scrap Fabric
- Weave or braid fabric scraps into a colorful, durable rug.

4 Photo Frames from Old Magazines
- Roll or fold magazine pages to craft unique, eco-friendly frames.

Holiday & Seasonal DIY Projects

1 Recycled Paper Gift Wrap
- Use old newspapers or magazines to create artistic gift wrap.

2 Eco-Friendly Ornaments
- Craft ornaments from pinecones, twigs, or salt dough.

3 Wreaths from Upcycled Materials
- Create holiday wreaths using fabric scraps, old CDs, or wire hangers.

4 Natural Air Fresheners
- Fill jars with baking soda and essential oils or create stovetop potpourris.

Appendix III: Interactive Tools

Sustainable Living Checklists

Living sustainably is about making thoughtful choices that reduce our environmental impact and promote a healthier planet. Whether you're just beginning your sustainability journey or looking to deepen your commitment, small, actionable steps can lead to significant change. To help you get started, we've created these practical checklists covering key areas of everyday life: energy conservation, water use, and eco-friendly shopping. These checklists are designed to empower you with simple yet impactful habits that contribute to a greener lifestyle. Use them as a guide, and remember that every step —no matter how small—makes a difference. Let's take action together for a more sustainable future!

Appendix III: Interactive Tools

Water Conservation Checklist

☐ Fix leaks in faucets, showerheads, and toilets promptly.

☐ Install low-flow showerheads and faucet aerators.

☐ Turn off the tap while brushing your teeth or shaving.

☐ Collect rainwater for outdoor watering needs.

☐ Water plants early in the morning or late in the evening to reduce evaporation.

☐ Opt for native plants in your garden that require less water.

☐ Use a dishwasher instead of handwashing (when fully loaded).

☐ Install a dual-flush or low-flow toilet.

☐ Reuse greywater (e.g., from washing fruits and vegetables) for non-drinking purposes.

☐ Use a broom instead of a hose to clean driveways and sidewalks.

Eco-Friendly Shopping Checklist

☐ Bring reusable shopping bags, produce bags, and containers to the store.

☐ Purchase items with minimal or recyclable packaging.

☐ Buy locally-produced and seasonal foods to reduce transportation emissions.

☐ Choose products made from recycled or sustainable materials.

☐ Avoid single-use plastics (e.g., straws, cutlery, and cups).

☐ Opt for bulk purchases to minimize packaging waste.

☐ Support brands and companies with transparent, eco-friendly practices.

☐ Buy second-hand items like clothing, furniture, and electronics when possible.

☐ Avoid fast fashion by investing in high-quality, durable clothing.

☐ Plan meals to reduce food waste and avoid impulse purchases.

Appendix III: Interactive Tools

Energy Conservation Checklist

☐ Replace incandescent light bulbs with energy-efficient LED bulbs.

☐ Unplug electronics and appliances when not in use.

☐ Use a programmable or smart thermostat to optimize heating and cooling.

☐ Switch to renewable energy sources like solar panels or wind energy, if possible.

☐ Seal windows and doors to prevent energy leaks.

☐ Wash clothes in cold water and air dry whenever possible.

☐ Use power strips for electronics to easily turn them off when not needed.

☐ Install energy-efficient appliances (e.g., refrigerator, washing machine, or water heater).

☐ Take advantage of natural light during the day.

☐ Use ceiling fans to reduce reliance on heating and cooling systems.

The **Sustainability Habit Tracker** and a **Sustainability Goal Planner**. These can help to monitor daily habits and set meaningful sustainability goals. The habit tracker includes daily tasks for a week, while the goal planner allows to outline specific objectives and track progress.

Habit	Day 1	Day 2	Day 3	Day 4	Day 5	Day 6	Day 7
Turn off lights when not in use	☐	☐	☐	☐	☐	☐	☐
Use a reusable water bottle	☐	☐	☐	☐	☐	☐	☐
Avoid single-use plastics	☐	☐	☐	☐	☐	☐	☐
Compost food scraps	☐	☐	☐	☐	☐	☐	☐
Use public transport or bike	☐	☐	☐	☐	☐	☐	☐
Buy local and seasonal produce	☐	☐	☐	☐	☐	☐	☐
Unplug appliances not in use	☐	☐	☐	☐	☐	☐	☐

Sustainability Habit Tracker

Habit	Day 1	Day 2	Day 3	Day 4	Day 5	Day 6	Day 7
Turn off lights when not in use	☐	☐	☐	☐	☐	☐	☐
Use a reusable water bottle	☐	☐	☐	☐	☐	☐	☐
Avoid single-use plastics	☐	☐	☐	☐	☐	☐	☐
Compost food scraps	☐	☐	☐	☐	☐	☐	☐
Use public transport or bike	☐	☐	☐	☐	☐	☐	☐
Buy local and seasonal produce	☐	☐	☐	☐	☐	☐	☐
Unplug appliances not in use	☐	☐	☐	☐	☐	☐	☐

Sustainability Goal Planner

Appendix III: Interactive Tools

The **Zero-Waste Home Audit Worksheet**. It includes sections for listing disposable items, reusable alternatives, and action plans for different areas of the home. This worksheet is a guide to identify and replace wasteful items with sustainable options.

Area	Disposable Items	Reusable Alternatives	Action Plan
Kitchen			
Bathroom			
Office/Workspace			
Living Room			
Bedroom			
Outdoor Spaces			

Zero-Waste Home Audit Worksheet

www.ingramcontent.com/pod-product-compliance
Lightning Source LLC
LaVergne TN
LVHW050026080526
838202LV00069B/6929